the Da Vinci Cold

Chicken Soup
for the
Renaissance
Man's Soul

BY L.K. Peterson

ILLUSTRATIONS BY
Randy Jones

Front and Back Cover by Randy Jones

For more on Now What Media Books,
please visit
nowwhatmedia.com/nowwhatbooks.html

Table of Contents

Introduction

Leonardo Da Vinci (1452-1519) was truly a
Renaissance Man. That he lived and worked
during the Renaissance makes it pretty much
a lead-pipe cinch. But even beyond the timing
of his birth he, like his peers (even more so,
his being a genius and all), sought to expand
humanity's knowledge and understanding of the
world.

Da Vinci accomplished this through his art
and in the stacks of notebooks he filled with
meticulously drawn observations of nature
and detailed plans for mechanical devices —
tanks, helicopters, the George Foreman grill —
centuries ahead of the technology needed to
build them. It is no small irony then, that one of
his greatest works of art is as noteworthy for a
calamitous technical flaw as for its artistic merit.

The Last Supper is one of the world's best-known paintings, second only perhaps to Da Vinci's other masterpiece, the *Mona Lisa*. Yet this iconic mural, painted directly onto the wall of the refectory (dining hall) of Milan's Monastery of Santa Maria delle Grazie between 1495 and 1498, began to fade and flake off almost as soon as it was finished and within a century of Leonardo's death was undergoing the first of many disastrous attempts at restoration.

What caused the mural's rapid deterioration has been a mystery for more than 500 years. But now, thanks to cutting edge technology, pure dumb luck and the perseverance of a shadowy, secretive organization, the amazing story behind this puzzle can finally be told.

Mostly.

2

Chapter One
The Germs of a Mystery

For centuries, scholarly debate about *The Last Supper's* deterioration focused on Leonardo's perplexing choice of materials; tempera and oil paint on dry plaster, instead of the traditional — and more chemically stable — fresco method of mixing tempera with wet plaster. Many also blame the additional long-term effects of the refectory's perpetual dampness and the harm done by clumsy restorers, to say nothing of the occasional war.

A small but annoying minority of researchers, however, firmly believed it was germs that had caused the damage. Specifically germs expelled by a sneeze — or even deliberately spat — onto the mural while the paint was still wet.

Derisively referred to as "Sneeze Theorists," reaction to both them and their ideas was usually "How did you get in here?" and "I'm calling security!"

By the late 18th century, frustrated by decades of being scoffed at as "cranks," "morons" and "doody-heads" by hidebound establishment academics with their "credentials" and "facts," the Sneeze Theorists, formed a shadowy and secretive organization known as the Association of Artists, Curators, Historians & Others Outcast ("AACHOO").

Today, more than two hundred years after its founding, this group is still so shadowy and secretive that its own members know little about it, each other or even that they are members at all. They meet only on February 29 of alternate leap years but are never told where.

AACHOO conferences invariably devolved into furious sectarian arguments over what (Head cold? Sinusitis? Allergies?) prompted the sneeze and who (or possibly whom) the offending sneezer might have been.

One faction hypothesized the sneeze came from Da Vinci's temperamental long-time companion, "Salai" (Gian Giacomo Caprotti da Oreno), who often behaved spitefully toward the maestro and whom Leonardo himself referred to as "a thief, a liar" and, occasionally, "Mary."

A rival AACHOO clique suspected the monastery's head abbot, with whom Leonardo had publicly feuded and threatened to use as the model for a waiter seen in the background spitting into the soup course.*

*Da Vinci removed this figure from the final composition.

Still another contingent proposed a "Second Sneezer Theory" as the only explanation for the extent and severity of the damage.

Clearly, these guys had way too much free time on their hands.

But the simple and frustrating fact remained that it could have been any of the dozens of people who were routinely in and out of the refectory during the years Leonardo worked on *The Last Supper*; including, most prominently, Leonardo himself.

For five centuries, these questions and others — although mostly the others — lingered in the air… until now.

Chapter Two
Who Moved My Sneeze?

The first hints of an answer came during the
most recent and extensive restoration of *The
Last Supper* that stretched from 1977 to 1999.
Toward the end of the process and after nearly
20 years of incessant pestering by AACHOO,
restorers finally allowed them to take a small
sample of the original for DNA testing, sighing,
*"Se farà questi scatti andare via, dia loro una parte
della pittura goddam."* ("If it'll make those jerks
go away, give them a piece of the goddamn
painting!")

Initial tests confirmed that, yes indeed, human germs consistent with someone suffering with a severe head cold were indeed embedded in the original pigment of *The Last Supper*. Further testing compared these germs to DNA samples known to be from Da Vinci (don't ask) and resulted in a 98.6% probable match. It was Leonardo himself who had sneezed onto the painting.

As startling as this news is to anyone who didn't see it coming in the previous chapter, these revelations raised as many questions as they answered.

Chief among these was why hadn't Leonardo, a compulsive record-keeper, ever mentioned his condition? In the 15th century, the common cold was a potentially serious illness, rating at the very least a "Dear Diary" moment.

The final pieces of the puzzle began to fall into place in 2005, with the rediscovery of a suite of rooms in Florence's Santissima Annunziata Monastery. With their fresco-covered walls, the rooms were long-rumored to have been Da Vinci's home in Florence from 1502 to 1506 but it was only after a close study of their contents and decor was Leonardo's residency there positively established.

The conclusive proof was a notarized letter tucked into a dusty notebook found at the bottom of an old trunk. Dated 1506 and addressed personally to Da Vinci, it was the landlord's refusal to refund Leonardo's security deposit, citing the lease's strict "No Fresco" clause and "stains on the carpet".

While the murals were quickly determined to have been painted by Da Vinci's students, the notebook became another matter altogether. After museum researchers moved the trunk into a climate-controlled "clean room" for study and begun to unpack its contents, they realized the notebook was gone.

Two years later came an astounding claim from America.

A notebook matching the description of the one missing from the monastery turned up in the possession of a Dr. Gerald Bostock, former Secretary/Treasurer of the North American chapter of AACHOO. Bostock presented himself as a "forensic art historian" but a Google search for the online university with which he professes affiliation resulted in a 404 message and its street address was a post office box near Bellevue Hospital in New York.

It would have been easy to dismiss Bostock's assertion as a hoax, except for the fact that the notebook was missing had never been made public and was a closely guarded secret among a small circle of Florentine museum officials.

Dubbed "The Bostock Portfolio", whether this notebook is the one from Santissima Annunziata and, if so, genuinely Leonardo's, how Bostock got hold of it (and exactly what kind of doctor he is, anyway), is at the center of an international storm of controversy, multiple lawsuits and a cookbook deal worth millions.

Bostock contends that this notebook is Da Vinci's own — indeed, the only — record of the cold that caused the sneeze that ruined *The Last Supper*, as well as containing Leonardo's secret journal of his dabbling in the medical and culinary arts in his effort to cure the common cold and make a couple of bucks along the way.

Because of ongoing litigation and a non disclosure agreement between Dr. Bostock, his publisher and the Food Network, our access to the material was limited to photocopies of sketches from the portfolio and selections of the text summarized from Bostock's own translation. He refused repeated requests for a sampling of the notebook's numerous recipes; reserving their revelation for the publication of his three-volume edition of the portfolio entitled, "Chicken Soup for the Renaissance Man's Soul: The Da Vinci Cookbook".

What follows, then, is the secret history of the Da Vinci Cold, presented in chronological order, except for the parts we already told you about, above.

Chapter Three
The Bostock Portfolio

MILAN, 1497

At the same time Leonardo was painting
The Last Supper, commissioned by his patron,
Duke Ludovico Sforza, the ruler of Milan, he
was also working on a larger-than-life-size
bronze equestrian statue of the Duke's father
and more popular predecessor, Francesco. Da
Vinci considered the statue more important
and interesting than the painting because of the
artistic, engineering and logistical challenges
it presented. When completed, it would be
the largest statue of its kind and the crowning

achievement of his career. Plus, it was a good way to kiss up to the boss (Leonardo knew which side of his bruschetta had the olive oil on it).

As the notebook reveals, working on both projects simultaneously took its toll. By early spring of 1497 Leonardo was physically and mentally exhausted. On the cool and rainy Good Friday of that year, Da Vinci awoke with a stuffy nose and a slight fever. He writes in that day's journal entry of having "...*sneezed all day while working on that accursed painting*" [emphasis ours] and complains bitterly about the dank refectory.

Still, no matter how lousy he felt, Leonardo was too far behind schedule to rest.

Periodically in his journals, Da Vinci mentions a neighbor, described either as "Dr. Morty" or

"The Spaniard," probably one of many Jewish refugees from the Spanish Inquisition who had fled to the relative safety of Milan. "Dr. Morty" is no doubt a pseudonym invented for his protection since he was the likeliest source of the cadavers Leonardo used in his anatomical research; something very much against Milanese law at the time, which deemed using the dead for scientific study as "Icky."

As his cold worsened, Da Vinci notes Dr. Morty's repeated offers to treat it with a hot broth of chicken and vegetables also containing "11 herbs & spices," that he called simply *sopa de pollo* (chicken soup).

Although skeptical about the efficacy of this humble elixir, Leonardo was finally persuaded by the doctor's logic, *"Non potrebbe danneggiare"* ("It couldn't hurt").

Da Vinci was relieved of his congestion so quickly and was so impressed that he begged for the formula of this *"minestra miraculoso"* (magic soup). Dr. Morty demurred, claiming it was a professional secret handed down from Maimonides' grandmother, telling the artist, *"A che cosa, Macy dice a Gimbel?"* ("What, does Macy tell Gimbel?"). While this statement puzzled Leonardo, he got the drift and backed off.

CHICKEN SOUP FOR THE RENAISSANCE MAN'S SOUL

Determined to recreate and even capitalize on Dr. Morty's soup, Da Vinci, a practicing alchemist and, by all accounts, an enthusiastic but abysmal chef, transformed his kitchen into a laboratory (or his laboratory into a kitchen; the phrasing is ambiguous) and began working feverishly. His cooking sessions lasted for days on end, during which time Leonardo neglected both the mural and the sculpture, emerging only when he believed he'd made a significant breakthrough.

Visitors to the refectory who'd come to watch the master at work were often treated to the result of his experiments. Da Vinci would seek out anyone in the crowd with the sniffles and foist upon them, sometimes rather aggressively, a cup or, for a lira-and-a-half more, a bowl of his most recent concoction. Because his intent was medicinal rather than culinary, the recipient's reaction was not always helpful. Many spectators who had initially arrived merely to watch paint dry came back for the free food. Those who'd sampled one of his less-than savory offerings, however, were not always so quick to return

Word got out about his experiments and in October of 1497, while at work in the refectory,

Da Vinci received a visit from a pair of burly "representatives" from Milan's powerful Barber/Surgeon Guild. The guild had a tight lock on all of the region's tonsorial and healing arts. Nobody in Tuscany stayed well-groomed or healthy without their say-so.

The unpleasant duo reminded Leonardo, in none-too-subtle terms, according to his notes, that the guild didn't take kindly to artist-engineer-inventor-geniuses horning in on its turf. They made thinly veiled threats, *"Mural che de Nizza avete ottenuto là; sia una vergogna se qualcosa accadesse esso"* ("Nice mural you got there; be a shame if something *happened* to it), to make sure he understood.

Furthermore, Leonardo's visitors went on to suggest, his failure to cease and desist his experiments, would not only guarantee he'd never get a decent haircut in this town again, but he could wind up in big trouble with the Tuscan Leech Guild, and you definitely didn't want to tangle with those bloodsuckers.

Leonardo assured them that he got their message loud and clear. Rattled but undaunted, he continued his experiments but now did so in secret, keeping his notebook hidden and writing in it not just backwards, but upside down as well.

FORWARD INTO THE PAST!

In the year 1500 Duke Sforza was overthrown by the French (this was back when the French not only fought but even occasionally won.)
By then, *The Last Supper* had been completed and the bronze intended for casting Da Vinci's

monumental statue had been "repurposed" as cannonballs in the futile defense of the city.

With his meal ticket locked up in a French dungeon and not anticipating a warm welcome — much less lucrative commissions — from Milan's new regime, Da Vinci hightailed the 200 miles south to Florence, the city of his youth.

By 1502 Leonardo had secured rooms at the Santissima Annunziata Monastery in Florence, where he tutored pupils in fresco painting and traded catty remarks with Michelangelo ("Little pisher!" "Washed-up old queen!"), who was now the rising star of the Florentine art world that he had once been and toward whom the older artist grew increasingly resentful.

Although he continued his chicken soup experiments during his stay (many of the sketches and recipes in the notebook date from this period), by the time Leonardo left Florence in 1506, his interest in the topic had fallen off considerably. A journal entry dated November 1505 states, *"Se non vedo mai ancora un altro pollo, sarà troppo presto,"* ("If I never see another chicken again, it'll be too soon").

Ironically, despite his inability to come up with a workable cold cure Da Vinci's cooking skills improved dramatically. Writings by his Florentine contemporaries often refer to Leonardo's talent for improvising a tasty dish on the spot from whatever ingredients he had just lying around — so long as one of them was a chicken. In 1503 and 1504, a dinner party at Da Vinci's was the place to be and of him it was often said *"Fa la destra del pollo!"* ("He does chicken right!").

Chapter Four

Selected Drawings from the Bostock Portfolio

26

[Figure 1]

Leonardo became fixated on the idea that an animal as perfectly stupid as a chicken could heal anything, and spent months slicing and dicing hens and roosters, using individual parts one at a time in various recipes in a process of elimination to scientifically determine which bits of the bird contained curative powers.

In a side note, Da Vinci hypothesized that animals' "intelligence" was in direct inverse proportion to their tastiness; i.e., chickens were dimwitted but delicious while humans were smart but tasted, well, foul. "Or, so I've been told," he was quick to add.

[Figure 2-5]

Never one to shy away from using himself as a guinea pig, Da Vinci kept careful records, including self portraits, as he passed through each stage of his condition.

[Figure 6-9]

Initially, the soup's flavor was of no interest to him, but Leonardo soon came to realize that if people couldn't manage to swallow the stuff or keep

it down once they had, it wouldn't be very effective
as medicine, so he began carefully recording crowd
reaction to each new attempt at a tastier recipe.

[Figure 10-11]

As practical as he was visionary, Da Vinci
began working up plans for commercial applications
for a cold-cure even while he was still experimenting

with recipes. This "Cavalry Officer's Field Kit for
Chicken Soup" was created in an effort to win a
lucrative military contract with the Milanese Army.

[Figure 12]

Da Vinci believed that a direct approach was best and drew up plans for methods of dehydrating his chicken soup, creating pellets from the powder, then propelling them directly into the nasal passages. This drawing represents only one of the many "delivery systems" he came up with and, like his miniature trebuchet and spring-loaded crossbow, was a painful and costly misfire.

Minestra di Polla

del Lisa del Mamma

[Figure 13]

Leonardo hatched a scheme to seal soup in used chianti bottles and market it to busy Renaissance housewives as ready-made cold remedy. Focus groups, however, found "Mamma Lisa's" enigmatic expression suspicious ("She's up to something. I don't know what, but I don't like it"), hated the slogan ("Good to the Last Schmaltz!"), and said that the decanted soup tasted like "Some chianti a chicken fell into."

Chapter Five
The Da Vinci Coda

THE AFTERTASTE OF A GENIUS

For reasons he took with him to the grave, when Leonardo departed Florence in 1506, he left behind the notebook, his recipes and much of his cookware. Perhaps he tired of his growing reputation as *"L'ospite con il la maggior parte"* ("The host with the most") or got fed up with people just "happening to drop by" around dinnertime.

There is even speculation that Leonardo deliberately ditched all evidence of his culinary achievements to hide what he considered an embarrassing failure or to ensure that his legacy wouldn't be bogged down by his efforts at something so prosaic. It may also have been his lingering fear that the Barber/Surgeon Guild would figure out what he'd been up to and turn him over to the guys with the leeches.

Then again, notorious for his short attention span and easily distracted, Da Vinci may have simply forgotten about the notebook before anyone else even knew it existed.

Whatever the reasons, we can be fairly certain that someone, somewhere is forming a shadowy and secretive organization to bicker about the possibilities and that we'll have the answer in a few hundred years or so.

www.ingramcontent.com/pod-product-compliance
Lightning Source LLC
Chambersburg PA
CBHW030523100426
42813CB00001B/129